Prologue

This tale is part of the history of a tiny village called Cambridge, located some 40 miles northeast of Albany, NY. The village was incorporated in 1866, but the "crossroads" has been inhabited since prehistoric times. Paleo Indians used a system of trails down the narrow valley, while others, coming up out of the Hudson River Valley to the west, followed a narrow defile into the valley, and camped on the banks of the Owl's Kill brook to trade and rest before continuing east thru the gaps into the nearby Green Mountains.

Cambridge was once more economically viable than it is today. The days when milk trains twice daily carried dairy and other farm products directly to markets in Boston, Albany and New York City are long past. Having long been denuded of the old growth pine grove that, with rail service, made Cambridge a "destination" for city dwellers seeking momentary respite from heat and congestion, the Village remains the size (2,000 souls) it has been these past 100 years.

While no longer a tourist destination, it is inevitably converting to bedroom community, to which down-staters repair for weekend and summer solace. Cambridge has always been a "one horse" town. Would it could stay that way. dt

Seeds & Plows

19th Century Industry
In the Old Cambridge District
by Dave Thornton

Contents

JB Rice Seed Co.	**p. 4**
Rice Mansion	**14**
Cambridge Steel Plow	**37**
(WA Wood Co.)	**55**
Images of Industries	**65**

In 1987, when the towns of Cambridge, Jackson and White Creek were preparing to celebrate the founding of the Old Cambridge District, from which they sprang, a few of us decided to prepare a book on the local history. As unofficial chairman of the endeavor, I sought out Lyman White, as the most experienced and knowledgeable man available, to tell the story of this community's greatest industry, the Jerome B. Rice Seed Co.

Mr. White was a good friend and tennis and squash-playing companion. He also had been president of the Seed Co. when it was a part of Asgrow.
A true servant of the community, Mr. White provided leadership and the seed co. facilities for many war-related projects during W W II. When in 1947 the Union School burned, he made the seed company facilities available for classrooms and administration of the district school. Mr. White was a founder of the United Fund and a prime mover in the buying and restoring of Hubbard Hall. In 1988 he remained a seedsman highly respected within the international industry, whose advice was widely sought. He died at the turn of the century.
The following is the narrative which he prepared and which I included in the 1988 Old Cambridge Book, which is long out of print.
The illustrations are largely from a collection maintained in the Old Cambridge Archive and Records Center,

which was founded, funded and built by the same people who produced The Old Cambridge Book. -Dave Thornton

Jerome B. Rice Seed Co.
by Lyman N. White

Nobody knows exactly when the seed business first came to Cambridge. It could well have been a result of the Shakers, who had colonies about forty miles south of Cambridge, growing seeds in the Cambridge area on the "farmer contract" basis. This method is still common in the seed business and we know that the Shakers were seedsmen.

In fact, the Shakers originated the system, which became very common, of leaving a box of packet seeds with a dealer in the winter, letting him sell from it in the spring, then picking up what was left after the planting season was past and being paid for what had gone out of the box. But it is only a surmise that the Shakers grew seeds in the immediate neighborhood.

However, we do know that there was a seed company in Cambridge as early as 1816. This was the Crosby firm, which was well know in the early nineteenth century. Crosby salesmen were peddlers, travelling from farm to farm by wagon and carrying the seeds with them.

H. Niles Rice started a seed business in 1832. This was in Salem, but his son, Jerome B. Rice, moved the business to Cambridge after the Civil War. He was fantastically successful and in the late nineteenth century the Jerome B. Rice Seed company was larger than any other American seed operation except D. M. Ferry & Co.

COMPLEX BUILT IN SWAMP

The Rice building complex was constructed near the railroad in what had been a swamp. The swamp was drained and Rice's Brook allowed to run through the middle of the property, with a miniature covered bridge, still in good repair, spanning it.

Jerome B. Rice was a cripple, due to illness contracted during the Civil War while in a prison camp, but he must have been a brilliant man. He organized the business and attracted many outstanding people to work under him.

Edwin Cornell probably knew as much about seed values as anyone in America. John L. Hunt, sales manager, was liked and respected universally. Ed Smith, treasurer, kept the company on a firm financial base. Charles Guelph was a legendary salesman, specializing on sales to other seed companies and to canners.

Probably the company reached its peak about 1900, when the present office building was built. Building No. 1, with its cupola and bell, had been built earlier-- about 1880. The wooden building, called "No. 2", was immediately behind Building No. 1. Buildings No. 4, 5, and 6 were warehouses and located behind Building No. 2. Warehouse No. 9 was built in 1917 on a railroad siding, east of Pearl Street. This big building is now the home of Bentley Seed Company. There were also Buildings 3, 7, and 8, torn down about 50 years ago, and Building 10, torn down more recently.

DIFFERENT KINDS OF COMPANIES

There are different kinds of seed companies. Some handle only grass seed, some only hybrid field corn, some ust grow flower seed which they sell to other seed companies, and some concentrate on sales to canners, freezers, and large commercial growers.

The seed companies that are best known to the general public are the ones with seed catalogs. But these are usually not as large as the wholesale packeters, which sell to dealers. The Jerome B. Rice Seed Company combined a wholesale packet seed business with sales in bulk to other seedsmen, to canners, and to dealers. It bought some of its seed and produced some itself on farmer contract.

Rice advertised its seeds as "northern grown" and this was usually true. But there was less in it than met the eye: most other American seedsmen could have made the same claim with an equal degree of truth. Except in California there was hardly any seed growing in the south and most seedsmen had their seeds grown in the same areas--beans in Michigan, spinach in Holland, etc.

Jerome B. Rice, Sr. died in 1912. From this time until 1939, when the business was sold to Asgrow, the story is not a cheerful one. There were still able men in the company but nobody was in strong enough position to keep it moving ahead. And there was nobody quite able to fill Jerome B. Rice's shoes.

Seed was sometimes sold too cheaply when it was in short supply. On the other hand, the farmer contracts were sometimes too large and big inventories of seed began to build up. There was an acute inventory crisis after World War I when European countries began to export seed again after not doing so during the war.

Probably all American seed companies suffered because of this but the Rice Company was in the most exposed position and was hurt the most severely by seed that had cost more to produce than it could be sold for. While it took twenty years for the company to fail completely, it never got back to where it was prior to 1919.

BEST YOUNG EMPLOYEES LEAVE

Some of the best younger employees left the company. Probably they sensed that the company was headed for disaster. It was decided that the main difficulty was lack of working capital and the company sold preferred stock to local people to raise money. It was done with the claim that the company was prospering so well that management wanted to share its wealth with loyal Cambridge citizens.

Quite a bit of money was raised and was largely used for things that did not need to be so expensive, like the sprinkler system. I think this took place in 1927.

There was a Rice family disagreement and partly because of it Jerome B. Rice, Jr. left the company along with George Coulter, a competent salesman, to found Jerome B. Rice, Jr. Inc. in Shushan. This seed company was active until the close of the century.

Finally, in the 1930's, the court appointed a receiver. This was David Ashton, who had been born in Cambridge. For manager he got Howard Earl, a respected seedsman. But conditions were already quite bad and a quick cure was impossible. David Ashton was succeeded as receiver by Spencer Eddy of Saratoga Springs. Howard Earl left and was succeeded by Harry Hoard and he, by Joseph Warren.

Conditions were going from bad to worse; the company was in Chapter I 1, and in 1939 the court sold the business for $20,000 to Asgrow. There was no equity left for Rice stockholders and not much for the Rice creditors.

During Asgrow's first two or three years at Cambridge there was a certain amount of local feeling that there must have been something crooked about Asgrow getting the company for such a small amount of money, while the Rice stockholders received nothing from the sale. The local stockholders were especially bitter.

And of course the Rice Company had been a local institution, while Asgrow's Cambridge operation was simply a branch of a company owned by Connecticut Yankees. Some of the Asgrow people in Cambridge believed that Jerome B. Rice, Jr. had spies in the Asgrow Cambridge office. My own guess is that there was no formal spying but a fair amount of local gossip, so that the Jerome B. Rice, Jr. organization did know what was going on. But it did not seem to hurt Asgrow.

UNDER BOTH ASGROW & RICE

My own experience with the Seed Company in Cambridge was entirely during the Asgrow period. At first we operated under both the Rice and Asgrow names; there was still a good deal of customer loyalty for Rice's seeds. Asgrow came at a good time, just before World War II, and was able to take advantage of the victory garden movement.

The Rice branch of Asgrow had some important customers, the largest being Sears Roebuck. Another customer for several years was Procter & Gamble, which used seeds as premiums.

The Cambridge branch was the packet seed division of Asgrow and the only part of the company that handled flower seeds to any extent. Old Cambridge residents will remember the flower trial gardens on Washington Street.

Many of the Rice employees became valued Asgrow workers. At the risk of being unfair because of omitting some names, it is still important to acknowledge the company's debt to Frank Knox, sales manager, and Tom Shiland, who took over as superintendent from Joe Arnold when Joe went to Connecticut.

Charles Clough was foreman of the "White Kitchen", where packets were placed in the displays, and in the summer he was a salesman in Vermont. All of these people contributed heavily to the success of Asgrow, perhaps Tom Shiland especially. Then there were some outstanding women: Sarah Arnott, Eva Vetal, and Madeline Wilson McWhorter, to name just three.

Among the people who came early in the Asgrow period but had not worked for Rice the following names stand out: Don Roderick and R. W. Richardson, salesmen; Leon Ridgeway, office manager and controller, who went on to perform the same functions for Asgrow's home office in New Haven, and John Lylis, sales manager. When Leon Ridgeway went to New Haven, Wilbur Martin filled his Cambridge position.

SEVERAL BRANCHES UNDER CAMBRIDGE

Asgrow had several branches that were under the Cambridge management. One of these was Indianapolis, organized mainly to take care of Sears in the Middle West. Norman Boyle was manager of the Indianapolis branch and did a great job as long as that branch was maintained. When it was closed he performed the same function in the larger branch at Sheboygan, Wisconsin.

Then there was a California branch, also primarily for Sears, and this was at first in Salinas, later in Downey and Los Angeles, finally in Azusa, California. Ray Bentley headed this branch for many years.

Asgrow was in the grass seed business for awhile and during part of this period Ray Lufkin managed a grass seed warehouse and packaging operation in Albany, Oregon.

During the latter part of the Asgrow period Ingemar Liljeberg was a strong force in managing the warehouse and factory. Olive Chesbro was a superb office manager.

In 1967 Asgrow bought the Mandeville & King Company, which specialized in flower seeds and operated out of Rochester, NY. The business was moved from Rochester to Cambridge during the season of 68-69. Shortly after Asgrow purchased Mandeville & King, Asgrow itself became a subsidiary of Upjohn, the pharmaceutical company. I was then close to retirement age and Upjohn hired T.T. Toole to be my successor when I retired. Actually he was the man in charge for about a year before my formal retirement in 1971.

It is probably fair to say that the packet seed business in Cambridge operating under the Asgrow-Mandeville name was larger in 1969 than it had been at any time since the First World War. But there were problems and the company decided to liquidate its packet seed operation in 1976. By then T.T. Toole had left and his successor, Robert Hamilton, was the manager.

USES OWN COLOR SEPARATIONS

Asgrow used its own color separations for packet pictures, having bought them in Europe during the 1960's. It subcontracted the printing to Excelsior Printing Co. of North Adams, then die-cut, folded and gummed the packets.

This practice was unique in the seed industry; but I knew it was cost effective, so when I retired from Asgrow in 1971, I founded the Cambridge Seed Packet Company. At the end of 1986, the company became Cambridge-Pacific, Inc., a subsidiary of Pacific Lithograph Company. It continued for a number of years to operate in the Cambridge area, selling packets to seedsmen in the eastern half of North America.

It has sometimes been said the Upjohn was interested only in the "write-off" of the Cambridge operation. This is less than fair to Upjohn. The company tried to make the packet operation work and certainly would have preferred a profit to a write-off. But it was a losing venture for some time and did not appear compatible with the main Asgrow effort, which was directed toward commercial growers of vegetables.

There is still a flourishing seed business in Cambridge: the Bentley Seed Company, which operated out of Rice's (and Asgrow's) Warehouse No. 9 until it burned. Since then they have raised a new building on the site. Just as there were many people who worked for Asgrow who had worked for Rice earlier, there now are many in the Bentley Seed Company who had worked for Asgrow.

WHY LOCATED IN CAMBRIDGE

Why has Cambridge been a location for seed businesses for 172 years? Originally seeds were grown in the Cambridge valley but for more than a hundred years now the amount grown locally has been insignificant; most of the seeds packaged here have been grown in the Middle West or Far West. Cambridge is not an ideal shipping point; it would be better if it were more centrally located. But it happened that Jerome B. Rice was a brilliant man and this was where he lived. For this and other reasons competent seedsmen gravitated to the area and apparently this was enough to make the Cambridge seed business flourish. After Jerome B. Rice's death there remained the seed processing plant and the people trained in using it. These are here today and help keep a seed business in the community.

An Old Cambridge Enterprise
by Dave Thornton

R. Niles Rice launched the family seed business in 1832 from a farm a few miles north of Cambridge. The headquarters was in Salem, NY. After the Civil War, the son, Jerome Bonaparte Rice, took over.

He moved the headquarters to Cambridge, first locating in the remains of an old steam mill that stood on Main St. where the West End Market is in the year 2,000.

In 1879, J.B. Rice conceived of bringing North White Creek and Cambridge Comers together by filling the swamp that separated them. A friend, James S. Smart, agreed to participate.

WCP BUILDING

Smart, who at that time owned the weekly newspaper The Washington County Post, bought a lot from the Blair family and built the famous newspaper building that stands today west of the Municipal Building. It was the first building in Washington County to be designed and constructed expressly to house a newspaper.

Rice built the first of what became a complex of buildings constituting the home office of the Rice Seed Co.

Writing in 1965, Elsa Parrish, widow of the local bank president, said that 3,000 loads of fill were required to raise the seed house grounds beyond the reach of the spring run-off. The brook that seeped through was ditched and walled, and became the centerpiece of the elaborately manicured Seed House grounds.

In 1888, J.B. Rice convinced the Village School Board to buy from him and build the Cambridge Union School on more raised swamp land, immediately west of his Seed Houses.

THE WATERWORKS, THE FAIR

In 1886, J. B. Rice pulled together a group of local business leaders to build the Cambridge Waterworks Company. In its day, it was a state of the art system, relying on a gravity feed, booster pumps and several hundred Irish immigrants to build it. Its most sustaining feature, of course, is its source: Simpson Spring, which to this day has not failed. For you see, the 100-year-old water system still services the homes of residents of the Village of Cambridge.

Then in 1890, J.B. Rice organized The Cambridge Fair. He bought out the failing, Lauderdale Fair, which ten years before the farmers and merchants of southern Washington County had organized around Lake Lauderdale, a glacial pond located five miles north of Cambridge Village at the head of the Owl's Kill Valley. Rice bought the Sanderson Farm on the northeast edge of the Village and founded what soon became the second largest Fair in NY State.

J.B. Rice's Fair should not be confused with "The WashingtonCounty Fair", which had been in existence since before the Civil War, and which The Cambridge Fair eclipsed. In its "hey day", the Great Cambridge Fair drew 10,000 visitors a day, mostly via chartered trains. Only the State Fair exceeded the premiums of The Cambridge Fair.

THE CHARTER
Neither The Washington County Fair nor The Great Cambridge Fair survived WW 11. After the War, a second charter was issued to The Cambridge Fair (the "Lake" charter). This charter was used to start up a county junior fair, which is what exists today in town of Easton (ten miles west of Cambridge) as "The Washington County Fair".

THE SEED GARDENS
The Rice Seed Co. provided bulk seeds for market gardeners and canners, as well as a great volume of packeted seeds for the retail market. There were trial gardens on Washington St. and on the Hitchcock Farm, which is now the grounds of Cambridge Central School, as well as elsewhere in this area.

In addition, the company came to have seed gardens in the Mid and Far West, in Michigan, Montana, Colorado, Washington, California and New Jersey. They also supplied seeds from Europe and Canada, even having a branch house in Wellington, Ontario.

In 1895, when the brick office building was added to the seed company complex, some 200 people were employed there, including a traveling sales force of about 30. The little family business in the Owl's Kill Valley of Upstate New York had become the second largest seed packet company in the Nation.

THE DEMISE
When J.B. Rice died, his son, J.B. Jr. was chosen as company president. But like many businesses, the company was hard hit by the depression. By 1934 the Rice Seed Co. was in receivership. J.B. Rice Jr. was let go as president, so he started his own packet business in Shushan, The J.B. Rice Jr. Seed Co.

The managers of the original Rice Seed Co. tried various ways to save it. They turned it into a stock company and sold shares, first nationally. In desperation, the officers tried to enlist the local community to invest in it. But it was too late!

EXTRACTED THE JUICE

Finally it was taken over by ASGROW (The Associated Seed Growers). Then, in the modem era of "buy-outs" by large corporations, the old Seed Co. was gobbled up, first by Mandeville and finally by the Upjohn Corp.

The latter extracted the "juice" and spat out the "pulp": The J.B. Rice Seed Co. became just so much local history!

VARAC PARK

Several years ago, a group of local businessmen watched the Seed House Complex begin to deteriorate. Determined to save it as a boon to the community, they purchased the complex. Four men were involved: The late Jim King, proprietor of a very successful local bakery; Fran Vitro, a printer; John Rich, the local hardware proprietor and Bo Anderson, who ran a metal casting business.

The investors did a great deal of renovation work, then recast it as VARAC PARK, a local industrial center. So. instead of becoming the rotting ghost of past local business triumphs, the former Seed House Complex is now a healthy part of the local economy

Since that time, they have become landlords to several successful small businesses that might otherwise not have been able to locate in Cambridge. In addition, following Jerome B. Rice's model for business acumen and dedication to the local community, these same businessmen have salvaged another nearby business complex; and a mile south of the Village they have established a classic industrial park.

The Rice Mansion
by Dave Thornton

But for the back-firing of a jalopy on Main St. in the wee hours of a cold winter night in 1930, the history of the JB Rice Mansion would be a good deal shorter.

Fortunately, this famous symbol of Cambridge's glory years did not disappear in the planned inferno, although she does yet bear scars from that dark night.

Thanks to the disturbed rest of a neighbor's maid, the mansion today joins The Cambridge Hotel and the Washington and Rutland Railroad freight houses as show-pieces in a general renaissance of the Cambridge Valley.

MAIN LINE VILLAGE

The turn of the 19th Century was a period of great dynamism in the Cambridge Valley. The railroad, constructed 50 years earlier, provided a main line link with Boston to the East and Albany and New York City to the West.

Two major industries flourished in the Village. The Lovejoy Furnace at the East End turned out horse-drawn farm implements, including their famous "Cambridge Steel Plow", that helped "break" the burgeoning West.

The other, The JB Rice Seed Company, was at its zenith. As the Nation's second largest seed packet operation, it supplied markets throughout the United States and Europe. The two families would become inextricably entwined on both business and personal levels.

Jerome B. Rice casts a long shadow over the history of The Cambridge Valley. Following his service in The Civil War, he turned the family seed business into an international enterprise. In 1886 he led the long-needed, but oft-thwarted drive to establish a Village Water Works. In 1890 he founded The Great Cambridge Fair, second largest in NYState.

He physically pulled together the two competing "corners" of North White Creek (Park and Main Sts.) and Cambridge (Main and Union) into a single cohesive entity. He accomplished this by buying and filling the swamp that lay between the corners, then building his seed complex on the fill.

Today a portion of that complex survives as an industrial Park. The waterworks continues to supply Village mains. Even his fair survives, as the Washington County Fair in Easton.

But this does not begin to suggest the breadth and scope of the business that the "Little Giant" built upon the beginnings of his father, or of its impact on the lives of Villagers of his day.

Suffice it in this essay to suggest that by 1900 Cambridge Village and the Rice family fortune were ready for a proper mansion.

MANSION CONCEIVED

At the urging of his wife, the "Little Giant" set out to build a monumental residence to reflect his success.

He chose a plot of ground adjacent to his growing seed complex in the center of Cambridge Village. At the time, he lived further west on Main St., but chose to build on the site of an earlier mansion that measured the early dominance in Cambridge history of the Crocker clan.

Indeed, at the time of the Civil War, when JB Rice joined in the Union Army as a lowly enlisted man, later to return as a lieutenant, the Crocker resident of that mansion would enroll as a Colonel and finish the war as a brevet General.

But by 1900 that Crocker was dead and his family moved away. Rice bought the land and had the mansion demolished. The carriage barn was moved to another location in the Village.

The Washington County Post, a newspaper that chronicled Village events from 1849, when it moved bankrupt from Salem, NY, until its own demise in 1986, provides the following account. The John S. Crocker mansion had passed into the hands of J.B's father, Niles. In the June 21, 1901 issue, the old WCP reported that the Crocker mansion had been torn down to make way for the residence to be erected by Jerome B. Rice.

It notes that the Crocker manse was made of "variegated blocks of color". "It was a marked feature in our Village," wrote the editor. "Almost as much so as the old Checkered House on the Turnpike."

The Checkered House, which burned in 1917, was also of the "variegated block" pattern, thought by some historians to have denoted an Inn.

By July 4th, 1901 the "rear extension" of the former Crocker manse had been moved off its foundation to the rear of the lot, so that construction on the Rice mansion could begin.

The Rice seed salesmen began their annual treks into the reaches of the Nation, while surveyors began laying out the plans for the mansion. Late in July a number of large trees were removed from the Rice lot, to allow for the construction.

LIBRARY BEGUN

At the same time, the community began a drive to raise a new building for a public library. This building may be seen today one block west of the Rice Mansion behind the Permanent Veterans' Honor Rolls.

By the end of August, the Rice seed sales force was returning to Cambridge, in time for the Fair.

At the time President William McKinley was being felled by assassin's bullets at the Pan-American Exhibition in Buffalo, workmen in Cambridge were completing the cellar and foundation of Rice's mansion.

The assassination of the president did not diminish Village attendance. Rice seeds were honored at the Exhibition with a gold medal.

By late Sept. the foundation of the mansion was complete. The WCP reported lumber for construction was "being piled up" on site.

Mrs. Williams, one of the George Law daughters, began the library drive with donations of $50 for books and $1,000 toward construction --- this at a time when $1,000 was worth $50,000 in modern sum.

In mid-October, the WCP announced that Horace Dodds of South Cambridge and his men had begun work on the frame of the Rice mansion, with the objective of enclosing it before winter.

FRAME IS UP

The frame was up before the end of October. Meanwhile, JB had the mound of dirt excavated from the mansion basement moved to fill more swamp behind the seed house.

By Nov. 1 the roof of the mansion was finished and ready for "the slaters". There had been only one day of rain since work began on the foundation, the Post reported. Charles Tierney was hired to slate the mansion. This work would progress slowly with the onset of a severe winter. The work was still not complete by the end of 1901.

LOVEJOY FOUNDRY

The Levant Lovejoys announced the birth of a daughter. Lovejoy was the heir apparent of the Lovejoy Foundry. His wife was one of JB Rice's daughters.

In early March, 1902, a carload of plows from the Lovejoy Foundry started south from the depot. The car was marked with a large banner, "Cambridge Steel Plows'.

No reports of progress on the manse appeared until May, when the WCP observed that "the elaborate ornamentation of the cornices of the Rice building" added much to its appearance.

In June, C.T.Hawley was building "a fine veranda" to his house at Broad and First Sts. In 2004, this was the home of Geoff and Christine Hoffer, proprietors of the Rice Mansion.

At the end of June came the report that work was progressing on the Rice mansion. "Exterior decorations are elaborate and handsome.... Everything is being done with marked care and with most liberal expenditure."

By the end of July, progress on the mansion had slowed "because of the time involved in putting on the exterior decoration."

In August, more shade trees were cut from the mansion lot. The current WCP editor, the Rev. John G. Smart, was no great lover of shade trees. From his newspaper office diagonally across Main St. from the Mansion, he observed that if about half of the shade trees on Main St. --- huge elms --- were cut the road mud would be lessened thereby. Main St. would not be paved with yellow bricks for several years to come.

It was soon Fair time in 1902. The Village loaded up with visitors. Special excursion trains dumped thousands daily at JB Rice's great fair. Production at all major enterprises in the Village ground to a halt. All employees were given fair week off (without pay, of course).

In September it was reported that the plasterers were finally at work on the interior of the manse. An "extended water tube is being sunk in the cellar for the hydraulic apparatus of the elevator."

C/W CASUALTY

It should be here noted that for much of his adult and most productive years JB Rice was wheelchair-bound by rheumatism. It is commonly traced back to his time of Civil War service. As a member of the 123rd NY Volunteer Infantry, he was in the Battle of Chancellorsville. There Thomas "Stonewall" Jackson led his rag-tag rebel army on a daring flanking movement that caught the Union forces by surprise and led to one of their worst defeats. Having just been placed in the front lines, the 123rd was one of the units that took the brunt of Jackson's assault.

Many local men were killed, wounded or captured. Rice was one of the captured. He endured a miserable winter in Libby Prison, Richmond, Va. before being exchanged.

He reentered service as a lieutenant in the newly created "signal corps".

BILLY WICKS

A colored man-servant, Billy Wicks, took care of Rice, including pushing his "cart" through the final years of his life. Rice built Wicks and his family a house on the Seed House grounds, where

Billy lived out his days. Both Rice and Wicks are buried in Woodlands Cemetery, Cambridge NY.

In early October, the Post reported that drilling for the elevator water tube was about finished.

At this time the bridge on Main St. over the seed house brook was so bad that the public was allowed to cross the brook through the grounds of the seed house and the adjacent Union School.

JB wasn't the only big business bug around Cambridge. George Law was another, albeit a generation earlier. That same October, Mrs. Laurence Williams, a daughter of George Law, gave another $1,000 toward the construction of a community library. It was her third such donation. Eventually she would pay for more than half of the total cost

The George Law descendents lived in season at Content Farm. The farm remains in the hands of descendents to this day. Before the Civil War, George Law was ranked among the top ten wealthiest Americans. He had spent his boyhood on a Jackson farm and was a typical 19th century success story: A self-made man.

Late in October, the Post reported that workmen hoped to finish the exterior of the mansion before the onset of winter.

That winter blew in early. By Dec. 12th blizzard conditions slowed work on the manse, as temperatures slipped to 30 below.

In late February, 1903, the remains of the old Crocker manse were moved from the Rice lot. It was the kitchen portion, used by the Crockers and later by Nathan Rice. It was moved to a lot owned by David Wells, who was to use it as a tenant house. The trees were so thick and the section so large that it was dismantled and moved in sections.

. Rice decided he wanted a terrace around his place. In March, draymen began drawing stone to the mansion site

[A side note: As a new water line was run from St. Luke's Place street for the current renovation of the mansion, the contractor --- "Tiger Bell" --- encountered a concrete foundation five feet deep and 2-4 ft. wide. Small wonder the fence has remained largely intact and unmoved for 100 years!]

In May, Rice announced that another huge warehouse would be added to the seed complex.

SOFT COAL

Painters were ready to put the first coat on the Rice mansion, but first they had to wash it! H.G. Clark, proprietor of The Cambridge, a hotel next door, had burned soft coal all winter to fight off its severity. Soot from the coal had coated the newly enclosed manse.

Soot from coal-fires steam engines was so bad that the Boston & Maine RR passed a rule restricting its employees from touching ladies' white shirtwaists as they helped them to and from the cars.

Laborers were busy building the "approach" and grooming the lawn.

The JB Rice Hose Co. was in the line of march that June, 1903, for the annual fire inspection parade.

The Union School Board of Education considered and rejected all construction bids, deciding to be their own contractor in building the new, Village Library. Levant Lovejoy's new, 10 horse power "Thomas" motor car arrived. It could carry five people.

"WHY I STOPPED!"

JB Rice Jr. acquired the first motor-cycle in the Valley. It was made by Marsh & Co. in Brockton, Mass., had a three HP engine and could reach a speed of 40 MPH.

Of course, greatly to the amusement of the general populace, he promptly had an accident. Kidded the old WCP: A new book is to be added to the Library --- 'The Motorcycle vs. The Woodpile" or "Why I Stopped", by Jerome B. Rice Jr.

A new law was added to the Village statutes that July. It forebade the riding of bikes (motorized or otherwise) on the slate sidewalks. Penalty was a $5 fine or 5 days in jail. Speed signs went up on Village streets. The limit: 8 MPH.

At the end of July, a hard rain spattered the fresh, red roof paint of the Rice Mansion over the railing around the east portico. Rice required that it all be done over.

The brick, stone, and slate for the new library was delivered that August. The committee asked donors to honor their pledges. Mrs. Williams was matching all pledges.

By mid-August the Mansion was painted and repainted and work began in earnest on the grounds.

Then suddenly it was fair week. Wednesday drew thousands, but Thursday's crowd was given as 12,000 --- double Wednesday's.

The WCP went "Ho Hum. Same old excellent fair!" JB Rice surely smiled.
Likely the editor did not fully appreciate the organizational genius Rice put into a fair that (in 1903) on Wednesday drew excursion trains from North Adams, Mass. (10 cars), Troy 13, and Whitehall 9. The four day attendance at the Great Cambridge Fair that year was given as 32,000!

The Post shed a tear as the last of the great trees was cleared from the Rice manse lot. It was an ancient elm that stood at the southwest corner, overlooking the intersection of Main and St. Luke's Place.

The giant did not go easily. The thunder of its falling limbs sparked two run-aways on Main St. Charles Cook's horse wrecked its harness and the wagon. Mr. McDonald's horse was caught without damage.

CRANKY EDITOR

The Post editor complained that the construction of the rock fence around the mansion was disrupting travel on Main St. "By the time the stone work is done on Rice's wall and the sidewalks can again be used, the mud will have frozen and it won't matter." Nothing that a dozen boards and ten minutes of work and a little authority couldn't correct, wrote the Rev. John Gardner Smart, who had succeeded his brother James as owner-editor.

That September brought the death of James S. Smart. A fellow C/W Vet, he had been a close friend and business associate to JB Rice.

Smart had shared Rice's vision of growing the two "corners" together. When Rice filled and built his seed complex in the swamp, Smart built on the corner opposite from where the mansion would rise. It was the first building constructed in Washington County solely to house a weekly newspaper, and continued through 2004 as the home of a printing business.

By November, the stone wall around the Rice Mansion was complete, as was the new warehouse over at the seed house grounds. Down Main St., the framing of the Library was finished and the roof was about to go on.

The Post did not let up on young JB Rice Jr. Having just returned from a business trip to Detroit, "Romie" set out on his motorcycle, "sighing for more wood piles to conquer."

The grading of the Mansion's front lawn was "progressing rapidly". Steps to the front entrance had been completed. Masons were at work on the stone posts of the driveway. The painters and decorators were almost finished with the inside.

By the end of November the wall and corner columns were complete.

FAMILY MOVES IN

Finally, the first week of December, 1903, JB Rice moved his family into the manse. Ever the businessman, he promptly rented his former residence to Mrs. Bosworth of Buskirk's Bridge.

By the middle of January, 1904, Rice was dazzling his section of the Village with the lighting around the Manse. Electric lights encased in glass globes sat atop stone posts at the driveway entrance, thereby "illuminating a hitherto dark section of Main and St. Luke's streets".

By the end of March the Post could report that the Library was complete.

In April, Edwin McClellan purchased the home of Mrs. J.J. Gray. He would rebuild it into a manse for his mother, Mary, and rename it "Meikleknox." McClellan would prove another great community benefactor. He would personally finance construction of Mary McClellan Hospital, which served the community until 2003.

After pulling down great trees in order to construct his new home, Rice began planting new trees on the grounds.

The sixth annual Field Day was held at the fair grounds that May. It is a little appreciated benefit of Rice having established the fair at Cambridge. High school athletic events --- football, track and baseball --- were played there for generations.

The first hard-surfaced road in White Creek was complete.

In July arrived the iron work to top the stone fences around the Rice mansion.

In July comes also the report that a cellar hole is being dug for the carriage barn at the Rice Mansion. The resulting soil is placed on the Library and Union School grounds to help to raise them above the flood plain.

LIBRARY OPENS

The Cambridge Village Library opened officially on April 25, 1904. The building cost $8,800. Mrs. Laurence Williams had given $6,800.

By fair time (which was again a huge success) the sidewalks and curbs at the Rice Mansion were completed. Rice even installed "a covered crossway" at St. Luke's and Main. Whether it sheltered Rice as Billy Wicks wheeled him across Main St. or across St. Luke's Place is unclear. It apparently didn't last long.

It was at this time that Rice had the sides of the brook that crossed the seed house grounds walled in stone.

By the end of September the frame of the mansion carriage house was up and ready for enclosing. By the end of October, Rice's "stables" were enclosed.

By the end of December, 1904, the carriage house was virtually complete; according to the Post, "making many residents envy the creatures for which it was constructed!"

Some small work continued on the mansion into the summer of 1905. Some curbing was added. The entrance gates were hung.

SOCIAL EVENT OF YEAR

Then in October of 1905, in what the editor of the WCP called "the social event of the year", the public was invited in to observe for themselves what the Little Giant had wrought! Wednesday evening, October 25, 1905, the Rices hosted 400-plus villagers. While 400 invitations were mailed, far more than that number showed up!

Far too many, in fact, for the mansion to accommodate them! A tent was set up on the back lawn, with a covered passage into the manse. The event was catered by a firm from Troy, NY. The carriage house was set up for dancing.

Doring's Orchestra from Troy played in the mansion from the second story hall. A second, unnamed (and therefore likely local) orchestra played for the carriage house crowd. The harness and tack rooms were lighted with jack-o-lanterns. Farm products completed the décor.

Cloak rooms were set up on the third floor, gents using the billiard room.

Guests were received in the room to the east of the main entrance. Receiving was by the Rice children and their college mates: JB Jr. and his sister Josephine; her friends Miss Hortense Fairman of Middletown, Conn. and Miss Milly Cross of Brockton, Mass. The Post noted many out of town guests, from NYCity, Albany, Boston, etc., as well as from the adjoining villages. Flowers were clustered in each room.

The Post called it "a brilliant, yet democratic gathering, which entered heartily into the conversations and gatherings of the evening.

"The chief adornment was the genial host and hostess and their happy family, and their rich hospitality will long be remembered by their guests."

That January, 1906, the Alumni Assoc. of The Cambridge Union School staged a production of the play, "A Call to Arms". Rice allowed his Civil War uniform to be worn by one of the caste. Harry C. Fassett was the lucky actor. The Post commented upon how "slim and slender" JB had been in 1862.

THE SEEDSMAN

There were several autos around Cambridge in 1906, even a rental agency ("autos to let. Prices reasonable"). JB Rice was not to be left behind. That May he purchased a seven passenger Pope-Toledo touring car and engaged Fred Spaulding of Salem as chauffeur. The vehicle would achieve 68 miles per hour, although not on the Cambridge roads of that day.

The purchase reflected his infatuation in innovation and technological advances. He saw to it that acts at his Fair were the very latest. Harness racing had to make room for primitive automobile acts and races. Flying contraptions of every description were staples of The Great Cambridge Fair.

Rice was sought for as candidate for the US Congress, but he regularly declined such solicitations. He was a seedsman, first and foremost. While Mrs. JB toured Europe, JB went to Toledo, Ohio for a Seedsman's convention

The "smooth, glassy" surface on the sidewalks JB put in front of his mansion caused several accidents the winter of 1907. The Post reported the need to keep the walks sanded.

In April, the National Express office in Cambridge brought in extra help to cope with the seed company's shipments. That October, the seed house would ship five railroad carloads of seeds to the US Dept. of Agriculture. The seed packets were to be given by Congressmen to their constituents.

THE VETERAN

That May JB was elected president of the Washington County Civil War Veterans. Mitchell McFarland, reporter and co-owner of the old WCP, was chosen Colonel. The next annual convention was to be in Cambridge.

In June, the Rice Mansion was repainted in "canary and white".

In August, 1908, the annual reunion of Washington County Civil War Veterans was held at the Rice Mansion. The 29th annual event was not as grandiose as in days gone by. Many Vets, like President Rice, were beginning to experience ill health. Many others were deceased. So, by past standards, it was a modest gathering.

The Washington County Post reported that Rice had a large tent set up on the lawn, with tables and seats. The East Greenwich Drum Corps attended, but there is no mention of the Cambridge Band, with which Rice had a love/hate relationship.

Rice led a parade of 52 Civil War Vets through the Village. Then the "president" of the Village, Charlie Tingue --- a retired old stage coach driver --- gave out meal tickets to The Cambridge (now known as The Cambridge Hotel). That stretched the capacity of the hotel, so the Drum Corps had to dine further down Main St. at the Union House (in 2004 the site of a used car lot).

The Post noted in a special tribute, that during the Civil War, the site of the reunion was the home of brevet Brigadier General John S. Crocker, who raised and then commanded the 93rd NY Volunteer Infantry.

Orderly Sgt. George Scott of the locally raised 123rd NY reported that of the 100 on the roll he used to call, only one --- himself--- was around to attend the 29th reunion.

Wives and girlfriends looked on from the Mansion porch as the Drum Corps concluded the event by "playing." Watermelon was cut and served.

Rice always tried to have the very latest forms of entertainment at the Fair each Fall. In 1908 he brought in an "air ship,, a lighter than air balloon powered by engines.

The fair remained strong, although somewhat discordant. Rice had replaced the very popular Floral Parade on the closing day with a cavalcade of livestock. But the livestock didn't have the general appeal of the young Cambridge ladies in their festooned carts and carriages.

The evening after the Bennington City Band performed at the Fair, they marched to the Mansion and serenaded JB Rice. Rice reciprocated by passing cigars all around.

SON-IN-LAW DIES

That November, Levant Lovejoy died. He was the only son of Henry H. Lovejoy and heir apparent of the Lovejoy Plow Works and husband to JB Rice's oldest daughter. A talented musician, a violinist graduate of the Boston Conservatory, and for a time a member of the Boston Symphony, Levant had dutifully come home from Boston to help his aging father. He had indeed turned the business around before he died of lung congestion. Tuberculosis was the most common killer in those days.

After the death of Levant, Frank P. Larmon purchased an interest in the Lovejoy Foundry and became its manager.

At the end of the September, 1909, came another elaborate wedding of a JB Rice daughter. Josephine married Frederick Wallace of Fitchburg, Mass. at the Cambridge Methodist Church. Wedding gifts included a Steinway Grand Piano.

In February, 1910, came the announcement of the engagement of JB Rice Jr. to Mary Rowe, daughter of the Methodist minister.

That October, the three key characters in the JB Rice saga, Mr. and Mrs. Rice and Billy Wicks, were involved in a carriage accident. They were ascending the hill into Brownell Hollow. Billy was driving. The single horse could not make the steep climb. JB, who was at this point wheel-chair bound, told Billy to get out and hold the horse. But the horse backed the carriage into the ditch, where it over-turned, penning Laura Chandler Rice between seat and top. They escaped with only scrapes and bruises.

END NEARS

In October, renovations to the Methodist Church were completed: The roof slate was fixed, the spire repaired, a chimney built up the west wall and the building repainted. The interior had been frescoed tan with oak leaf borders. George Peters, who for many years painted fair advertising for JB Rice, did the interior painting.

Green and brown Brussels carpet was added. The oak pews were redressed and upholstered. Cherry and oak fittings were added for the pulpit and choir. A cement step and new oak doors were added at the front.

JB Rice was entering his final days. He was not going to leave his church in disrepair.

In February, 1911, JB Rice Jr. married the parson's daughter. George Peters created the foliage that decorated the altar. The bride's only "ornament was a ring of diamonds and sapphires, a gift of the groom." The bride's father, Rev. HS Rowe, performed the ceremony. They would tour Egypt, Turkey, the Holy Land, and other points in the Middle East.

By May, JB Sr. and wife had returned from a Cuban tour. He was thought cured of the illness that had befallen him during the winter.

That October, the Post reported the 70 yr. old JB Rice to be ill at the mansion.

In late winter, 1912, Rice went into the hospital in Baltimore for bladder surgery. From his bed, he would have followed the death throes of the Lovejoy Foundry, as it went into bankruptcy. Both his son in law Henry and his wife Evelyn Rice, had to file.

Frank Larmon, who had joined the Lovejoy company after Levant Lovejoy died of a heart attack, now followed other directors into bankruptcy court. His indebtedness, like theirs, stemmed from signing notes as a director to keep the company going.

Rice survived his hospital stay and went south with his son for the benefit of a warmer climate. They returned to Cambridge in May.

In May, the Lovejoy Foundry was sold for $20,000.

STARS FALL

Then, like stars falling across the night sky, prominent residents began to die. First came word that Mrs. Laurence Williams had died in her suite in the Plaza Hotel, NY City. Her body lay in state in "The Little Church Around the Corner" in NYCity and was then borne by a four car special train to Cambridge for her burial in Woodlands.

Then Robert Alexander Maxwell died. Born in Jackson, he rose to be the State's first Insurance Commissioner. He also served as State Treasurer and assistant Postmaster General. He joined Mrs. Williams in Woodlands, his burial plot but scant feet from JB's.

DEATH CLAIMS CAMBRIDGE'S "LITTLE GIANT"

Finally, on Saturday, June 8, 1912 Jerome Bonaparte Rice departed life. The Post obituary included the following particulars:

The son of R. Niles Rice and Betsy Ann Hodges had been born in Salem July 19, 1841. He was educated in district schools and Albany Business College, from which he graduated at the age of 19.

When the Civil War broke out, he was working on his father's farm in Jackson. He enlisted from White Creek on August 8, 1862. He mustered into Federal service in Salem that September as a private. He shortly was made a sergeant in Co. G, the 123rd NY Volunteer Infantry.

He became a prisoner of war at the Battle of Chancellorsville on May 3, 1863. He was confined to Libby and Belle Isle prisons, before being exchanged on August 1, 1864.

After being exchanged, he transferred to the new Signal Corps. There he served as a lieutenant in the Dept. of the Cumberland under Gen. Thomas until the close of the war. He mustered out in Albany on June 27, 1865.

After the war he returned to his father's seed farm. In 1868 he bought out R. Niles and continued in the farm and seed business. For two years or more he was his own sales force, traveling by horse and wagon from town to town.

In 1868, he moved the business to Cambridge, occupying the second floor of the old steam mill on West Main St., the foundations of which remain in use to the present time, in 2004 supporting the building known as West Village Market.

Rice operated from there for 11 years. Then in 1879 he bought Robert Coulter's swamp and completed his first warehouse there. In 1895 he added a fine office building in front.

At the height of his success as a seedsman, the JB Rice company was the second largest in the nation. Rice employed 25 book-keepers and stenographers. His 30 salesmen traveled throughout the United States.

In addition to his Cambridge gardens, Rice had trial gardens in the west, the upper mid-west and the south. He had branch offices and warehouses in Detroit, Michigan and Wellington, Ontario. Eventually his company would also have one in Southern California.

HONORED BY PEERS

In 1898, Rice was honored by his peers in the seed business. By acclamation, he was elected president of the American Seed Trade Assoc.

His exposure to the elements during the Civil War and his resulting imprisonment were seen as the causes of the severe rheumatism from which he suffered. . Year by year it grew more crippling, until at the time he built his mansion, Billy Wicks, his colored manservant, had not only to dress him, but also to push him about in his "go cart."

This, the Post noted, rendered the more notable his great achievements in business. The list must highlight the JB Rice Seed Co., The Cambridge Waterworks and the Great Cambridge Fair, for in each, his was the pivotal role in its success.

It was in July of 1877 that Rice married Miss Laura Chandler. Together they raised four children: Three daughters were Mrs. Josephine Rice Wallace, Mrs. Evelyn Rice Lovejoy and Miss Marguerite Hodges Rice; one son, JB Jr. At the time of his death,

Evelyn had presented JB with one grand-daughter, Betsy Rice Lovejoy.

His body lay in state in the entrance hall of the mansion, which over-flowed that Wednesday afternoon for the funeral.

The following week, the Fair Board met and selected John L. Hunt to be its second president.

That same June saw the Lovejoy Foundry rising like the Phoenix from the ashes of bankruptcy, to become "The Cambridge Steel Plow Co."

That fall, for the first time in its history, The Cambridge Fair was lit by electricity. How JB Rice would have loved that innovation!

That January, 1913, JB Rice Jr. was elected to the board of The Cambridge Fair, filling the seat formerly held by his father. John L. Hunt was continued as president.

In April, 1913, a second floor piazza was built onto the back of the Rice Mansion.

Friday, May 2, saw the arrival of the first rail car load of yellow brick for the paving of Main St.

In a quiet, late May ceremony, JB Rice's daughter Evalyn, the widow of Levant Lovejoy, became the wife of Dr. Frank G. Schaible of NYCity. The groom was organist at St. Luke's Episcopal Church and a practicing physician in NYCity. [Note: In those times, the Williams sisters made St. Luke's a very wealthy Church. They hired the best singers for the choir. It is not much of a stretch to see them regularly bringing from the City Dr. Schaible to play the organ.]

JB Rice Jr. seemed unable to rise to the stature of his late father. In Hoosick Falls that June, Rice drove his automobile into Miss Alice Cuddihy, who stepped off the curb in front of it. Again, the Post had some fun with it, writing that Rice "was paroled in his own recognizance." Nonetheless, that July JB Rice Jr. was elected president of the seed company.

The 1913 Cambridge Fair featured "captive balloon rides."

That October, The Cambridge Band led the first parade on the Village's almost complete "yellow brick road". In the annual fire inspection parade, the Band was followed by 13 men of the Rice Hose Co.

That July, 1914, Joseph McWhorter and his crew painted the Rice Mansion.

FURTHER TRAGEDY

In early November, 1914 another major tragedy befell Mrs. Rice. Her nephew, Edgar Chandler, was driving the automobile that collided with a train just above the Village, resulting in the deaths of all four of the young women riding with him, two of whom were his sisters. Since the fast, hard roads were put in, three had already died in train-auto collisions at that crossing, but none so horrific.

Chandler ran a clothing store in the Village. He would physically survive the accident, but would close his Village business and move to Albany.

Mrs. Rice went south for the winter.

That February, 1916, Lyman Chandler of Greenwich, Mrs. Rice's father, died of a cerebral hemorrhage. Chandler had been a salesman for the seed co.

With the leadership of "The Little Giant" missing, in 1916 the Cambridge Fair yielded up the first sign of decay. A State report revealed that for the first time EVER it slipped below the county fair in state rebate money for premiums paid out. The county fair received $4,000; the Cambridge fair $2,898.

Because of the spread of "infantile paralysis," children under 16 were barred from attending the Fair that Fall. Attendance dropped from 23,000 in the previous year to 13,000 in 1916.

On July 4, 1917, members of the Masonic fraternity lay the cornerstone of the new hospital.

The Cambridge Band furnished the music at the Cambridge Fair that Fall. Governors from both Vermont and New York were scheduled to attend.

The year 1918 was dominated by WW I: Sacrifices on the home front --- shortages and restrictions and war bond drives --- and lengthening casualty lists from Europe.

That March, for the first time in history, Village women voted in the annual Charter election. Frank Richardson was reelected mayor.

LAURA CHANDLER RICE

That May Mrs. JB Rice Sr. was reported to be critically ill of pleura pneumonia, likely brought on by the influenza pandemic. Two daughters came home to assist her, Mrs. Josephine Rice Wallace and Mrs. Frank Schaible, both of NYCity. Her nephew, Edgar Chandler, visited from Albany. . The following week, she died.

By the time Laura Chandler Rice passed the Nation was consumed with news of WW I and was decimated by a great influenza pandemic. As leader of the community, forward had stepped Edwin McClellan. After establishing his mother, Mary, in Meikleknox on S. Union St. and himself internationally in the patent medicine business, he gave to the community Mary McClellan Hospital. It was opened early to help the community cope with the influenza.

Mrs. Rice was the daughter of Edgar D. and Sara Everetta Chandler. She was born at Hartford, NY on July 22, 1854. Her family came to live in Greenwich.

She was active in civic and philanthropic affairs, and was active in the Methodist Episcopal Church. Of course, she was an officer and one of the principal stockholders of the JB Rice Seed Co.

Mrs. Rice was survived by her children, a sister, Mrs. Evelyn Fleming of Greenwich and her brother, Edgar Chandler.

Shortly after the death of Mrs. Rice, the mansion was repainted.

That June, Marguerite Rice, the youngest daughter of the JB Rices, married Dr. Harry Lambert Collins of Chicago. They expected to live in Chicago.

In July, Mrs. Josephine Rice Wallace shipped to France as a canteen worker, helping the US Soldiers there engaged.

The concrete wall along the seed house brook was re-laid. It had been damaged by frost heaves. Thomas Conklin did the work.

To help the hospital staff cope with the epidemic, on Saturday, October 26th a women's auxiliary was formed.

In late January, 1924, Cambridge lost another major benefactor when Edwin McClellan died of a heart attack while in London. His body would be returned by Cunard Liner to Cambridge for burial in Woodlands Cemetery on the hill already occupied by JB Rice and other prominent citizens.

RICE SEED GOES PUBLIC

That May, Rice Seed Co. entertained 100 employees at the Cambridge Hotel. Pres. John L. Hunt and other officials encouraged the workers to invest in the business. Hunt told them that the company's "growth was out-stripping the growth of its working capital."

The company offered an issue of 4,000 shares of preferred stock at $20 per share.

Two nights later, the Seed Co. hosted 150 local citizens, who were invited to the same "banquet feast."

But in fact, the stock offer was a desperate effort to save the company from failure.

It was 1924. In five years things were going to get a lot tougher for the aging company. But in the meantime, employees were organized into teams and a contest begun to see who could sell the most stock. The winner's prize: Five shares of Rice Seed Co. stock.

The employees had every reason to participate. In a week they sold 1,531 shares and bought 863 shares, themselves. This brought in $47,880 in fresh capital for the ailing company.

The company bought the remaining stock and proffered it at $21 a share, through brokers. In another week, the workers had sold or bought 7,443 shares, bringing in $148,860 REAL dollars to the company.

That May that a new front porch was built on the Rice Mansion.

BUILDER DIES

In April, 1925, the builder of the Rice Mansion died. Horace Dodds of South Cambridge died of old age (he was 87) and gangrene of the leg. He was a leading carpenter in the region for 55 years.

That July, the WCP announced that two JB Rice daughters, Mrs. Schaible and Mrs. Wallace, were summering in Europe.

In August, JB Jr. was elected to the Village school board. By 1925, JB Rice Jr. headed the Seedhouse.

But in 1926, more money problems surfaced in the Seed Co. Henrietta Howe brought suit in favor of her late husband. She sued Rice Seeds for $25,000. Seems in 1918 the troubled company brought in Frank Howe, a financial expert, to straighten out the problems. He was appointed managing director, given $125 a week and promised $25,000 when he finished the job. Apparently the other directors didn't think his work merited the final payment, so they did not pay it. He began the suit before he died. In February it was announced that the widow settled with the Seed co. for half of the sum promised. One more "nail" in the seedhouse "coffin."

After the death of Laura Chandler Rice, the Mansion remained largely unoccupied. No Rice child claimed the Manse as her residence; so, in 1928 JB Jr. sold it to two NYCity men. According to the research of Peter Bell, LLS, Charles A. Forcey and Theodore A. Reynolds were the purchasers, in the name of Reynolds-Forcey Co. Inc.

Times were at the moment "booming". Likely, they saw it as an investment opportunity.

According to Surveyor Bell, Forcey-Reynolds closed on the Mansion on Sept. 28, 1928. Almost a year later, in October, 1928, the stock market crashed and the Nation began the spiral into the Great Depression.

FLAMES ON 2ND FLOOR!

Tuesday night, September 30, 1930 an attempt was made to burn the vacant Rice Mansion. The alarm came at 3:15 AM, given by Miss Bridget Killeen, employed by the family of A.B. McNish, whose mansion stood opposite the Rice home on St. Luke's Place.

Judging from the description preserved in the pages of the Washington County Post, it was the work of a "professional." All that saved the mansion was its location --- across the street from the Firehouse --- and the sound of a poorly timed automobile. It backfired repeatedly as it drove up Main St. This roused the McNish family. When their servant, Miss Killeen, went to the window of her second floor room to investigate, she saw flames behind the windows of the second floor of the Rice Mansion.

Since the firehouse is just across Main St. the main piece of fire apparatus at that time --- the chemical truck --- was on the scene almost at once, according to Fire Chief William Wells.

The fire laddies needed an hour and a half to subdue the blaze, which was fueled by an accelerant. Chief Wells said that upon entering the second floor of the vacant home, a 30 gallon drum of gasoline was found sitting on the floor of the open hall. Packed around it were bunches of blazing sacks. The barrel was prevented from igniting, thus saving the house.

Wells said the walls and door casings had apparently been drenched with gasoline. The paper was blistered and hanging loose from most of the walls. The casings around the doors and the woodwork around the stairways were badly burned.

Glass in doors and windows was smashed largely by the fire fighters, Wells said, in their effort to reach the flames. The interior of the house was "badly smoked up!"

Under Sheriff Alexander and a State Trooper began an investigation which turned up more evidence. They found ten five gallon gasoline cans thrown over a bank on the Cambridge-Greenwich road this side of the Ambrose Kelly residence. The cans were all new, some wrapped in burlap and some in paper, while some were unwrapped, reported the old Washington County Post.

The barrel was filled with 30 gallons. The presumption was that the other 20 went to saturate the walls and door facings and stairs. The firemen left the 30 gallon drum of gasoline in place.

Then, the next night, Wednesday at 2 AM, another fire broke out! ---this possibly from smoldering remains. But again, the firemen intercepted it and quelled the growing inferno.

At that time of the arson attempt, the Rice Mansion was owned by Charles A. Forcey and Theodore A. Reynolds. Workmen had been repairing the Mansion recently, wrote the Post.

Almost exactly one year after the crash --- two years after Reynolds-Forcey acquired the property --- a professional arsonist set fire to the Mansion.

CHECKERED PAST

From the purchase of the Mansion in 1928 until the present, the house was not owned by a Rice. Indeed, its history as a residence is quite checkered. It has served longer as a "play-house" for curious Village boys than it has as a residence.

According to Mr. Bell, the property came into the hands of Malcolm M. Parrish of Cambridge, Washington County Treasurer, for failure to pay taxes. In August of 1933, Mrs. Lena F. Reynolds paid the arrears and reclaimed the property for the payment of seven hundred and thirty-two dollars and 72 cents.

The property remained in the Reynolds family until they sold it to Joe and Janith Sourdiffe in 1958. For several years, they operated a restaurant on the first floor of the Manse. It was popular with the more affluent and style-conscious of the local community.

The property was sold to Rebecca S. Griffin in 1968, the restaurant operation ending at about the same time.

In 1975 it was conveyed to Charles and Dawn Pollock.

In 1984 the Mansion was again sold, this time to Don and Eileen Darling. They converted the Carriage Barn into rental suites. The Mansion housed their office. They extensively reworked the Carriage Barn and hired some rehab work on the Mansion, mostly on the exterior. The interior remained sufficiently attractive that several prom coronations were held there while the Darling children matriculated at the local Central School.

After their last child graduated, the Darlings left the area. After the space of two years, during which the Mansion was vacant, Geoff and Christine Hoffer purchased it. While their plan of historic restoration and preservation is unfolding before your very eyes, they continue to operate the mansion property as a "bed and breakfast" inn, with a view toward expanding the number of available suites and making the Mansion a "living museum", as nearly as is possible like it was when Jerome Bonaparte Rice Senior opened it to overwhelming public response way back in October, 1905.

The Cambridge Steel Plow
by Dave Thornton

THE CAST-IRON PLOW

The plow that Broke the sod of the West was invented right here in Old Cambridge. It is this early invention that the Warner and Lovejoy plow-works capitalized upon.

According to Scientific American Magazine of 1876, Jethro Wood took out the first patent on a cast-iron plow. Until Wood's invention, sod and loam breaking plows were sticks of wood plated with iron beaten into shape at the blacksmith's forge.

WHITE CREEK BOY

Wood was born in White Creek in 1774. A State historic marker at the site of his farm can be seen along the highway half a mile south of White Creek Village.

It was Wood who conceived of a plow to be cast whole from molten iron. He patented his plow in 1814, but he did not make a fortune.

Indeed, his invention suffered from its very significance, for his was one of those insights so profound that no amount of patent law could prevent its universal application for the general good. Lawsuits he brought against those who infringed upon his patent soon broke him. Wood died a poor man in 1834.

At the time, Secretary of State Seward said of him, "No man has benefitted the country pecuniarily more than Jethro Wood; and no man as been as inadequately rewarded."

In 1879, H.K Fisher, a poet, who grew up in White Creek, recalled Jethro Wood, and the life of the early plowman.

There were several styles of plowing. Generally the plowman started with a strip in the middle of the field, and plowed subsequent rows around it until he reached the edges of the field. Sometimes a plowman would start on the outside and plow to the middle. This gave a change for the team and threw the soil away from the stone walls, leaving a ditch to the outside.

Another technique was "laying out"; that is, back furrowing.

SIDE-HILL

In hilly regions, such as the slopes over-looking the Owl's Kill Valley, another invention, the "side-hill" plow, was preferred. The contraption allowed a plowman to swivel the plow share to compensate for the slope.

Like Secretary Seward, Fisher underlined the significanse of the invention of the cast-iron plow. It revolutionized agriculture.

Fisher grew up on a farm next to that of Jethro Wood and recalled boyhood observations of the inventor, seated on horseback with a long-handled fork, leisurely spreadinghay.

Wood spent much time on horseback. Fisher recalled seeing him eating peaches directly from the tree, with both of his hands in his pockets.

"Poetry, as well as agriculture, is much indebted to lazy men," concluded Fisher.

Fisher remembered that the Wood plow, while a breakthrough, was not the perfected form that gained National fame as "The Cambridge Steel Plow". The Wood plow of his boyhood was easily clogged and hard for team to draw "and man to grind". But it was greatly in advance of what Fisher's grandfather had used.

Fisher noted that since the days of Jethro Wood, inventors have produced instruments adapted to all types of soil. "However high the weeds, the Gale or Oliver plows will bury them beyond redemption."

GREAT VARIETY

They came with "handles that adjust to the smallest boy or the tallest man, moldboards of chilled metal; a joiner and coulter attached, of light drafts and which never clog. These plows seem to be as nearly perfect as possible."

He found both the Gale and the Oliver to be popular in Western New York, as was the Remington ---"ideal in light soils, and easy to handle". But for clay soil in a dry time "there is no plow as good as a Ward".

He did not mention the local product at all; but then, at the time of the writing, he had long since propelled himself onto the Frontier.

The Plowman's mighty labors demanded hearty food. Fisher recalled that for breakfast, he would likely consume aloaf of rye or Indian bread baked in a brick oven and brought smoking to the table, with potatoes, coffee, maple syrup, ham and eggs.

MAIN MEAL

The main meal was called dinner, not "lunch", and occurred in the middle of the work day. The Plowman would consume a huge hunk of the same brown bread baked fresh that morning, a chunk of boiled, corn-fed pork, a dish of greens and "bag pudding", to be eaten with sugar and cream.

"Such fair sent the farmer to the field to wield the fork, swing the scythe or hold the plow."

He recalled a corn planting jingle: "One for the blackbird, one for the crow, one for the cut-worm and three to grow!"

Blackbirds were the nemesis of the corn farmer, as in those days they wheeled into the planting fields in great flocks. "Nothing but a shotgun on hand availed with them," he recalled.

PLOWING CONTESTS

In the "old days", implement dealers would pit their products against the competition in head-to-head competitions.

In July, 1879, on the Hiram King farm in Town of Cambridge the W.A. Wood mowing machine took on the Champion (with its front gear design) and the new model of the Buckeye". In a test of draft (drag), using Baldwin's dynamometer, the National standard, Woods machine pulled at 168 lb., the Buckeye at 196 and the Champion at 209.

But in a trial in heavier grass, over a 100 ft. pull, the wood mower lost, drafting 201 lb. to the Buckeye's 196 and the Champion's 209.

Wood's agent was running the contest, and he was not at all satisfied with the second result. He set up another trial in lighter grass. The Wood got its 168 lb draft, and the other two machines were not allowed another run.

Business is, after all, "business"!

ON SWEET FARM
There were other such contests over the years, one on the Sweet farm in White Creek in 1881, where the Wood machine took on a McCormick and a Minneapolis; the names alone sufficient evidence that the farm implement industry had already settled on the Great Lakes in the Heartland of the burgeoning Nation.

EDDY VS. CAMBRIDGE
In 1895, the Cambridge Steel Plow was put to work in a contest head to head with the plow manufactured in Greenwich by the Eddy Plow Works.

The equally venerable Eddy Plow Works of Greenwich was dissolved in 1923 and taken over by James Leary of Saratoga Springs. In 1948, when the former Eddy Plow Works was sold to Eastern Tractor Manufacturing Corp of Kingston, NY, it had 40 workers on the payroll.

The bias of the WCP reporter who observed the plow contest can be forgiven. He claimed victory for the hometown, Lovejoy product, although the report in the Greenwich paper credited the Eddy plow with victory. The WCP reporter noted that the Lovejoy plow did not clog in the muck, as did the Eddy plow.

CAMBRIDGE VS. OLIVER
In 1899 another contest is recorded. It took place on the Alexander Sherman farm, Town of Cambridge, where the Oliver "chilled" plow went head to head with "The Cambridge". The outcome was judged by the farmer, "with the result that Mr. Sherman bought the Cambridge plow"!

WARNER-LOVEJOY
The plow manufactory was begun in 1844 by Solomon W. Warner. The Warners moved down from Salem and located on what was called the Beebe Block. This was just north of the Village Green at Park and Main, probably about where the present Church sits.

The Warner family farm is a mile north of Cambridge Village on that segment of the old Cambridge-Lauderdale Rd. The barn was used for a time by L'Ensemble as a music hall.

Solomon Warner took E. Robertson as partner, but in a year he sold out to Levi Tilton, who continued a year. Then Tilton sold back to Warner, who operated alone until 1850.

LOVEJOY PARTNER

At that time, only four hands were needed to run the operation. But in 1850, Warner took Hiram Lovejoy into partnership. Lovejoy was at that time making and repairing wagons.

They moved their expanded operation to a lot near Rice's Blacksmith shop and added steam power. Soon they needed eight hands.

Warner and Lovejoy stayed at that location until 1860, when they moved to their best-known location, on the brookat the mouth of Ash Grove.

At first the Foundry produced plows and stoves. But stove-making proved too competitive. Troy was becoming a national center for iron working, including a booming business in producing wood and coal burning heaters.

A few locals did make good in the early days of the stove business. The Ingrahams of Center Cambridge, at one time had a stove works at Troy.

IMPROVE STOVE

In the winter of 1813-14 William T. James of Cambridge improved on the design of Abbott's Square Stove. He patented the idea. The son of a neighbor farmer, Latham Cornell, went in with him. They formed the firm of James and Cornell. They made some stoves in Cambridge, then moved to Lansingburgh.

Known as the James or Saddlebags Stove, it was a popular item for a number of years.

In 1819, Nathaniel Starbuck of Easton, a blacksmith; with his brother Charles, also of Easton; and a Mr. Gurley of Troy, established a foundry. They cast some stoves for James and Cornell. Then in 1866 they were located on Starbuck's Island, on the Hudson River near Troy.

But the Warner Foundry, early on, found their niche in farm implements. In 1859 only four hands were needed to operate the plant. In June of 1863 the Washington County Post reported that Warner and Lovejoy had a furnace, shops and other buildings, and had added a saw and planing mill directly over the Ash Grove brook. They were making circular saw mills, water wheels, mill gearing, shafting, pulleys, corn and plaster crackers, grist and flax machines, and all kinds of farm implements and castings.

INDUSTRIAL BOOM

Charles Dudley Warner returned from the Civil War to take an active interest in the Foundry. In July, 1868, Solomon Warner died. Solomon and several others of the clan lie buried in the Park Street Burying Ground.

At the death of Solomon, his shares passed to his son Charlie, who then bought out the aging Hiram Lovejoy.

The business boomed during and immediately following the Civil War. "To those who a few years ago were familiar with the little stream that winds its way along down that narrow valley...," wrote a reporter for the Old Washington County Post, "A visit at this time among those old hills would astonish them.

"Where at the time was nought heard but the little stream as it glided swiftly along its stony bed, now are heard the roar and splash of the huge water wheels and the steady buzz and humof the various machinery that bespeaks of skill, industry and thrift."

The Mills of Ash Grove were making farm implements and utensils and grinding grain to flour and feed.

"While we haven't the water power of our neighbors..., what we lack in power is made up in enterprise."

Of course, the machine that drove local industry, as well as industry throughout the Nation, was The Civil War!

In August, 1868 he bought out the interest of Hiram Lovejoy, and in January, 1869 Charlie Warner sold half of the operation to Higgins for $15,000.

This was at the height of the post-war "Boom", when prosperity appeared to extend forever into the future. But in just two short years inflation, fed by war-fueled government borrowing, would stifle industry and drive the economy into a devastating depression.

During the Civil War, Charlie Warner had been quartermaster sgt. for the famed "Washington County Regiment", the 123rd New York Volunteer Infantry. The 123rd saw its share of action, including bearing the brunt of "Stonewall" Jackson's famed flanking movement at Chancellorsville.

The Regt. made the full march with the army of General William Tecumseh Sherman, from Chattanooga, Tennessee to the sacking of Atlanta, Ga., and on to Savannah on the Atlantic Ocean.

THE CASUALTY

Charlie Warner had dodged his share of minnie balls in the Civil War, but would be a casualty of the Depression of 1872.

But in 1869 things were going so well that the Foundry had 25 full-time employees. The company was doing more than $100,000 worth of business a year ($2 million in modern money).

By December, 1869, the Foundry was owned by C.D. Warner, in company with M.A. Higgins. They also operated a large sawmill from the same plant. Later they brought in a third partner, Solomon Green.

Aside from the charcoal required for the smelting, the operation waswater-powered, operating largely seasonally on the flow of the Ash Grove Brook and on run-off captured in large reservoirs east of the Brook. In 1997 these old reservoirs were still intact, although empty.

All machinery for implement making, the planes, lathes, etc. were contained in a single room on the ground floor of the main building. The carpenter shop and a storeroom were on the second floor. The molding room was a wing off the machine shop.

Shafts conveyed power to the blacksmith in another building.

LARGE FORGES

The Foundry boasted two large forges, and one smaller. They had a powered draft, which was adjustable. There was machinery for threading bolts and nuts, etc.

In 1869, the mechanic in charge was W.P. Harwood.

In 1870, Warner, Green and Higgins were doing business as the Empire Machine Works.

In December, 1871, Higgins sold out to the other partners, and the Foundry continued as Warner and Green.

CIVIC SAVIOR

In the history of the Cambridge Fire Dept. the name of Charlie Warner is ensconced amongst the Immortals. The Founder was J.J. Gray, but the "Savior" was Charles Dudley Warner.

By late April, 1871 the conservative "do-nothings", coupled with Hard Times had brought Cambridge Village to a stand-still. The Village had incorporated in 1866, largely to provide the twin hamlets with fire protection. The Trustees had bought a hand pumper and organized an engine company, known as the J. J. Grays, even putting up a building to house the engine. But by the spring of 1871, even the Engine Company was comatose.

Then the Village revolted. Solomon Fuller took over as President. C.T. Hawley was elected clerk, replacing the incumbent, "who got but one vote".

NEW TRUSTEE

Charlie Warner was one of the freshly elected Trustees. He found the firemen totally disorganized.

An example of just how bad the Dept. was can be found in the history of May 4, 1871. At 4 a.m. that Wednesday, The Union House was discovered to be ablaze. But by the time the boys had hauled the JJ Gray through the rutted streets, "amateurs" had doused the flames with an old-fashioned bucket brigade.

Charles D. Warner, Foundry heir and Civil War veteran, stepped in and reorganized the firemen.

Warner was made foreman of the Engine Co. And the first thing he did was order members of the old company to turn in their uniforms.

In early June the Trustees accepted Warner's reorganization of the Grays, and appointed R.A. Coffin chief engineer.

But even with Warner's leadership, the Grays failed to pull off a triumph when Ackley's Hall caught fire. A leaking kerosene chandelier went up during the performance of a touring show. Some scenery behind the drop curtain caught, and it looked to the audience as if the whole stage was afire. But it was quelled with little panic in the third floor audience, and little damage, "except that the soprano fainted".

But things were turning around for the Grays. Even if they could not star in their primary role as fire fighters they would succeed in a secondary role, that of fire muster competitors.

PUMPER CONTEST

Charley Warner pumped enough vitality into the Grays that they decided to go to a fire muster at Rutland for a July 4th competition. The Eagle Bridge and Washington Railroad connected through to Rutland. The boys drilled regularly. Charlie brought the venerable hand pumper into the embrace of his talented mechanics, who soon had it in top condition.

The first of a string of historic victories came at Rutland that July 4th.

That summer of 1872, Charley Warner and his new partner, Green, cast a 400 lb. cannon at their foundry, to be shot off at rallies of both political parties. It had a 2 1/2 inch bore.

Glory rained upon him! Charlie Warner was lionized for his brilliant rejuvenation of the Fire Dept. and his civic leadership.

The J.J. Grays were at the heighth of their success in competitions at fire musters. Little wonder, then, that at the annual election of the Grays in January, 1873, Charles Dudley Warner was continued as foreman ofthe Engine Co.

Never one to sit on his laurels, Foreman Warner formed a Hook and Ladder Co., to be known as "The Warner Hooks". It was the third company ever formed in the Cambridge Fire Dept.

Then, as the Grays were relishing their celebrity and fame at the fire musters, their credibility as a fire fighting entity was knocked out of the box by a classic, one-two combination.

TEST OF FIRE

The north side of Cambridge Corners burned. Down went the venerable Union House, and Harper and McClellan's huge new warehouse just west of it. Estimates of damage ran as high as $50,000.

Editor Smart pronounced the Fire Dept. "wholly inadequate", although the Grays did drag out "lots of stuff".

That was the "one". Two" was when Charley's own business burned. The Warner and Green Foundry burned the first week in January, 1876. The main building contained all of the machinery and patterns, all of which was destroyed.

The foundry, started a generation before by old Solomon Warner and carried forward by the young Civil War veteran C.D. Warner, was in ruins. Damages were estimated at $34,000.

The JJ Grays were decked and humbled. They had the best contest Engine in the Northeast in the J.J. Gray. They were the toast of the summer firemen's musters. And yet, they couldn't stop a fire at the business of their biggest supporter.

But they weren't out. They voted to incorporate themselves, and to buy a ladder truck. One was available from Bennington for $35. So the Grays were now an Engine Co., a Hose Company and a Hook and Ladder Company.

In May, the newly authorized Hook and Ladder Co. voted to name themselves after the man who had so rejuvenated the JJ Grays and led them back to glory, Charles D. Warner. For a few years they would be known as "The Warner Hooks".

But, alas, the flame of fame is fickle; and a civic leader but one whofinds himself in front of a community that happesn to be going the way he is. As quickly can they go the other.

So it was with Charlie Warner and the community of Cambridge.

INSURANCE MONEY

At the beginning of 1877, a controversy developed when the Village Board reviewed losses due to fire within the corporate limits in the year 1876. The total was $39,650, $23,000 of it being covered by insurance.

The three fire companies were to share part of the insurance money kick-back, which was based upon their effectiveness at preventing losses due to fire. The sum to be distributed to the fire companies was $90 ($1,800 modern).

The initial plan was to share it on the basis of the number of members in the companies.

The JJ Grays, breaks men and hose men, favored this; for being the largest company, it would give them the greatest portion, 2/3rds of the money, based upon membership.

But the Warner Hooks sought a 50-50 split, arguing that the Hand Pumper required large numbers to do nothing more than man the "breaks".

The Village clerk, himself a Hook, agreed with the Warners and paid the money on a 50-50 split. But the Village Board decided that they should have made that decision. Serving at the whim of the majority, it is understandable that they would reverse the action of the Clerk and declare for the Grays. The Board gave the Grays the bigger cut.

But the money had already been paid out!

TRUSTEES ACT

The Trustees ordered the Hooks to pay back to the Village all above their allotted sum of $30, but the Hooks refused.

They published a nasty note in the Old WCP, stating that they would not because the Board was making it look like they had done wrong, instead of merely accepting what they were given.

In their public letter, the Hooks asked the Trustees to apologize. Instead, the Village Board disbanded the Hooks.

Then the Board, by resolution, exonerated from any deliberate wrong-doing Clerk Shortt, the son of the Presbyterian minister.

The WCP declared the Hooks to have been wrong. Take it as a lesson, the Editor advised. He also suggested that the Board reorganize the Hooks, calling the episode "a boyish escapade by the Hooks".

The Hooks caved in and reimbursed the Village.

As "their continued suspension would be detrimental to the interests of the Village," the Warner Hooks were reenstated at the next meeting of the Trustees.

Although Charley Warner was no longer the "fair-haired boy" of the Village Board, he was still quite popular with his "Hooks".

In gratitude for their show of character in the dispute, Charley presented his boys with a magnificent, stuffed eagle, which they "acknowledged with a public resolution in his favor".

Then, bolstered by their Founder's support, the Hooks sent a public letter to the Board, declining reinstatement.

FUTURE LEADER

At that time, John Larmon had concluded his term as Washington County Sheriff, had bought into a local business and moved from Eagle Bridge, purposing to make Cambridge Village his permanent home. He would prove to be the next "savior" of the Fire Dept. Indeed, in later years, the Company founded by Charley Warner would bear the name of the "Larmon Hook and Ladder Co."

But in the meantime, Decoration Day, 1877 found the Gray Engine and Hose Companies joining with the Coila Band in the annual parade. Even though their founder and leader was due all honor on that solemn day, the Warner Hooks had to participate "unofficially".

At that time, the western migration was in flower. O.K. Rice of Greenwich (J.B. Rice's brother), as agent for the Union Pacific Railroad, offered half price excursions west to look at land. The verdant, unbroken sod of the Great Plains sold at that time for from $2 to $7 an acre. Anyone who bought 160 acres or more got his train ticket refunded.

The American Frontier must have looked terribly enticing to Charley Warner.

PRODUCTION SAGS

The economic depression drove production down until the Foundry only employed 12 men.

So, one moonless evening, Charley Warner packed his carpet bag, slipped quietly out of town and took the "down" train West.

Into the wilderness of Idaho he went, using contacts and his Civil War service record to get a fresh start as an Indian Agent.

Warner went west with the son of R.K. Crocker, who had published the Washington County Post during the Civil War. In January, 1880, B.D. Crocker wrote of their experiences on the Nez Perce reservation, following the Chief Joseph War. Warner was chief agent at Lapwai, Idaho Indian Territory.

Crocker told of loping on horseback through miles of virgin forest. It was like a vast park, with trees 6-7 ft. in diameter reaching the heighth of 70-80 ft. before the first limb.

He told of peering into a vast canon (canyon) where unsullied streams of sparkling water tumbled past deer and grizzlies feeding in plain view.

The Indians, those that could be coaxed from lucrative horse stealing along the Salmon River, lived in low, log huts: "One room, three beds and lots of people".

He saw them in the evening by lamplight attending Catholic worship. And he watched Charlie Warner distribute to the Indians their "annuities" from the Federal Government.

17 BLAST FURNACES

Drawing on ore from mines in the Adirondacks and fuel prepared from the forests east of the Hudson River, a vast smelting empire had sprung up by the 1880s. At one time there were 17 blast furnaces operating between Fort Edward and NYCity, with one in Cambridge, others in Hoosick Falls and a greater number around Troy.

They operated with a combined capital estimated at $8.5 million (in modern currency, conservatively estimated at $170 million).

But by June of 1885, the number operating in the Corridor was put at "three".

NEW OWNERS

By March, 1882 the Foundry had recovered, and was doing business as The Empire Machine Works. The owner was A. Walsh.

But in October, 1884 it was failing again. James Ellis took the failing enterprise from Walsh. Ellis held a $4,000 mortgage against the Furnace. Then Walsh, who was a brilliant machinist, leased it back and continued the manufactory.

In September, 1885 the Foundry passed back into the hands of the Lovejoys. With L.P. Worth as partner, Henry Lovejoy bought the operation for $4,800. Henry Lovejoy was the son of Hiram, who had owned the Foundry with Solomon Warner in 1850. He was a master machinist, like his father.

Worth had retired from the ancient jewelry and cutlery firm of Worth and LeGrys, which continues on W. Main St. in 1997.

In June, 1886, Worth dropped out of the Foundry business and Henry Lovejoy carried on with the support of Walsh.

LOVEJOY BOOMS

Under the industrial genius of Henry Lovejoy, the Foundry achieved a success surely equal to that enjoyed during the Civil War, when every Furnace and Foundry in the north was busily engaged in turning out war materiel.

At the Lauderdale Fair in September, 1887 Henry Lovejoy exhibited a line of implements of his manufactory that compared well with that of the Eddy Plow Works of Greenwich.

Local wagon and carriage makers also showed their wares: McGeoch and Pierce of Greenwich and Harrington, Galbreath and English of Cambridge.

By 1898, Henry Lovejoy was marketing a complete line of farm implements, including the world famous "Cambridge Steel Plow". Among many other implements, the Foundry offered "The Ellipse Corn Planter (Finest in the World!)" and "The Empire Wheel Harrow (The lightest draft harrow made, original and new)". It was spring tooth, with a seat and raisable running wheels.

That Fall, the Foundry received a special order for 500 plows from a "Down East" firm.

Anticipating a good spring of 1899, Lovejoy added five car loads of harrows, cultivators and planters to his stock.

Walsh had developed a very successful regulator for water wheels. The Fall of 1899, the Foundry made shipments of the regulators to such exotic climes as Brazil, Russia and Japan.

On a March afternoon in 1902, the "Down" Train coupled on a boxcar loaded with plows from the Lovejoy Foundry. The car was decorated with a large banner, proclaiming, "Cambridge Steel Plows!"

LEVANT LOVEJOY

Levant H. Lovejoy was born in 1874 and died in November, 1908. The son of Henry Lovejoy, Levant was a gifted violinist. He began is music development with the Cambridge master teacher, G.K. Nichols, who taught him both cornet and violin. Levant went on to study violin in Boston, graduating from the Boston Conservatory and playing for some time with the Boston Symphony

His marriage to Evalyn "Lena" Rice, JB's oldest daughter, united the two leading industrial families of the Village.

After marriage, Levant gave up his dream of a career in music to take over sales in the Lovejoy Foundry. It was largely upon the promise of Levant's great talent for promotion and sales that Henry expanded the operation.

It was, therefore, a fatal blow to the Lovejoy fortunes when Levant died young of consumption.

Frank Larmon, a son of John Larman, married Levant's sister. Larmon would eventually assume a leadership role in the management of the Foundry. An engineer educated at RPI, Larmon evidently did not possess Levant Lovejoy's gift for sales.

In 1910 the Foundry received another blow. In 1907 A. Stanley Rice had become Lovejoy's partner. His father, the late Alexander H. Rice, had been governor of Massachussetts from 1876-79.

But Rice died in January, 1910, providing another set-back leading tothe failure of the Plow Works.

It was about this time that Henry Lovejoy bought the Barr house on W. Main by Seed House Brook. He would spend the latter years of his life there, serving on the Village Board and taking on other civic duties.

FAMOUS SON

In August, Henry experienced a dangerous accident while cutting a pattern on a trip hammer. A sheet of glowing iron, fresh from the furnace, flew up and struck him on the brow. The one lb. piece of fiery metal burned his brow and shattered his spectacles, driving glass through the lid into his eye ball.

The emergency man, John Costello Jr., helped him to the doctor. It was fortunate for Henry Lovejoy that visiting his parents, the Dr. Harry Blackfans, at that time was Dr. Kenneth Blackfan.

Kenneth Blackfan had grown up in Cambridge, but already was well on the way to international fame as a pioneer in the field of pediatrics. He provided sterling emergency care, and Lovejoy was taken to an eye specialist in Albany, and he recovered.

UNIONS COME

Then labor problems hit. Thirteen men were employed in March, 1911 when they walked out on strike. They had been ordered to work a 10 hr. day, when they had been working nine. And, heresy of heresies, they wanted their daily wage increased to reflect the extra hour.

In response, Lovejoy shut down his line and offered the manufacturing of his entire line of harvesting machines to the W.A. Wood Co. of Hoosick Falls.

Strike breakers were brought in, but weren't needed, as the 13 men quickly decided to go back to work under the old terms.

FINALLY, BANKRUPTCY

In November, 1911 an involuntary bankruptcy proceeding was brought against the H.H. Lovejoy Co. of Cambridge, "one of the oldest manufacturers of plows and farm implements in the county". The company had assets of $61,000, with liabilities of $76,000. The action was brought by creditors: The Albany Trust Co., Manufacturers Bank of Troy, First National of Greenwich, People's Bank of Salem, Farmers National of Granville and the Cambridge Valley National Bank.

At a Nov. 9 meeting, the Lovejoy directors admitted a state of insolvency. The co. said the cause was a lack of business.

Perhaps it was Hard Times. Probably it was mounting competition from the great manufactories sprouting in the "Rust Belt" around the Great Lakes.

A month later employees were back at work, trying to keep things going.

That same December, Charles Lovejoy of Shushan opened a chaplet works on the second floor of the Fred Dwinnell building (in 1997 the West End Market). Eventually, this business would move to the Foundry works.

NO BUYERS

The directors found times hard. They had no buyers for the Foundry. The entire output of the plant was being marketed by the W.A. Wood Co., which would itself fall into bankruptcy after being one of the largest implement manufacturers in the Nation.

Henry Lovejoy's widowed daughter-in-law was Evelyn Rice, the eldest daughter of Jerome. B. Rice, who built the Seed House into the second largest in the Nation. But J.B. was in failing health, and the Seed House, too, was facing hard times.

There was nothing for it but that the daughter of this great local capitalist should join her father in law in bankruptcy court. Both were officers and major stockholders in the Foundry. Henry's liabilities totaled $54,000 (about $1 million modern) and Evelyn's $53,000. Mostly it consisted of their personal notes drawn to support the company.

The W.A. Wood Co. was having its own problems. But so much larger was it that sheer momentum would carry it years further into the new century.

Arrangements were made that the Wood Co. would market the Cambridge plows. Wood Co. sent a force of salesmen to the Foundry to observe a demonstration of the plow, prior to starting to sell it.

Frank P. Larmon now followed the family into bankruptcy. His liabilities totaled $46,000; for he, too, had been a company director, and had endorsed company notes to help the firm.

Receivers were Hiram J. Stevens and Frank C. Curtis. They collected $50,830 to apply toward the indebtedness of the firm. For their efforts, they received $545 in commissions. The attorney, Charles S. Aldrich, received $400.

SOLD OUT OF TOWN

In May, 1912 it was announced that after 70 years of local ownership, the Foundry had sold lock, stock and entire plant, to James M. and Inman E. Stower of Burden, Columbia County, for $20,000. A group from Granville had bid against them, but couldn't make the price.

The Stowers were well set up to take advantage of the marketing prospects of The Cambridge Steel Plow, as they owned the Hudson River Ore and Iron Works at Burden. They had probably learned of the opportunity from their cousin, Edward S. Anson, a Village coal dealer.

The old management was completing a 400 plow contract for the W.A. Wood Co. On June 15 the new owners took over. They immediately hired Henry H. Lovejoy to run the plant.

So, from the ashes of the bankrupt Lovejoy Foundry emerged that same June the bright Phoenix of "The Cambridge Steel Plow Co., incorporated with the State of New York at $100,000 capital. The directors were J.D. and J. N. Stower, H.H. Lovejoy of Cambridge and C.G. Nibblett of Hudson.

SHUSHAN CONNECTION

A second son of Hiram Lovejoy was Fred C., who died in February, 1923. He was born in Cambridge in 1858, son of Hiram and Alcesta Hall Lovejoy. In 1879 he moved to Shushan and in 1881 married Miss Julia Potter of Rutland, Vt. They lived in Shushan, where he founded the Lovejoy Co., manufacturing stove specialties. He was always in this "chaplet" business. He went from Shushan to Albany for 10 years, thence to Rochester for four, then back to Shushan. By 1919, the Cambridge Steel Plow Co. was defunct, and Fred Lovejoy was able to buy the Foundry facility. From that time he conducted the Patent Specialty Supply Co., moving in 1920 to Cambridge to reside.

The Patent Specialty Co. lasted almost to WW II. But shortly after Fred Lovejoy's death, the business passed to a Hoosick Falls firm.

DISTRIBUTOR CAPS

In July, 1940 the Hoosick Engineering Co., Inc. occupied the plant at the mouth of Ash Grove. E.H. Benway, Supt. utilized ten men and three "girls" for the manufacture of automotive distributor caps. The caps were made from Bakelite and were molded on two machines under 125 pounds of pressure per square inch.

In 1997, the business operated as H.E. Ignition.

CULLINAN BUILDS

Edward Cullinan was the master machinist in the Fred Lovejoy chaplet works, but he did not want to move to Hoosick Falls with the business. At the height of the depression, in 1933, when Cambridge Village was in desperate economic condition, Edward Cullinan convinced the more progressive businessmen of the community that he could start up and operate at a profit his own hinged tube and chaplet works. With their backing, Cullinan did just that. His hinged tube and chaplet works came to be housed in a factory building on S. Park St. The Cullinan company thrived during WW II, when it obtained government contracts to make parts for bomb sights.

Upon Edward's death, the company passed to sons, Gardner and Stewart, who continued it long after the war.

HENRY LOVEJOY

In December, 1931, the Cambridge Chamber of Commerce received a request from Dearborn, Mich. to furnish them with a history of the Warner-Lovejoy Co. As part of Henry Ford's famous museum of farm implements, a famous CAMBRIDGE STEEL PLOW was included. Henry Lovejoy was retired to his Main St. home and getting on in years. He furnished a history of the company, but could not find a catalog of the company's products.

In an interview given a little before his death, when Charles John Stevenson, editor of the old WCP, asked Henry Lovejoy for the most significant thing he had done in his life, he did not point to the plow works. Instead, he pointed to his vote as a Village Trustee to pave Main St.

When others wanted asphalt, Lovejoy had held out for the yellow bricks; which, at the time of his death in 1944 at the age of 94, had served for 30 years.

A Short Sketch...

Walter A. Wood MOWING AND REAPING MACHINE WORKS

(Provided by Hoosick Historian Joe Holloway)

The difference in scale of operation between the Warner-Lovejoy Foundry and the Walter A. Wood Mowing and Reaping Machine Works of Hoosick Falls is so great that the operations cannot be seriously compared: That is not my object here.

Today we enjoy the quiet life in sleepy, northeastern New York hamlets that the World has passed by. My object is to help the reader see these sylvan hills and sleepy valleys when the frenetic clamor of raw, industrial enterprise claimed them.

Consider, therefore, the magnificent, mowing and reaping machine works of Hoosick Falls.

FIRST MACHINE

Walter Abbott Wood introduced his first mowing and reaping machine in 1852, and began their manufacture in Hoosick Falls.

Wood was by training a blacksmith, having once worked at that trade in a shop that stood near the buildings along the Hoosick River in the Village that in 1874 housed an international machine works.

According to an account carried in the January 31, 1874 issue of the old Rensselaer County Standard, the First W.A. Wood mowing and reaping machines were built in that small blacksmith shop, later replaced by the foundry building.

Wood soon purchased Tremont Mills, which had been across the road from his first shop. Tremont Mills was a four story brick building, but soon was not adequate for Wood's expanding enterprise. He next leased Ball's nearby shop.

Wood operated that way until the eve of the Presidential election of 1860, when a fire, starting in Ball's shop, swept it, Tremont Mills, the Foundry, the scratch shop and the office, destroying everything.

But Wood built a new shop in time to fill most of the orders of that season.

STOCK COMPANY

In 1866 a stock company was formed, with Wood as president; William B. Tibbets, vice president and secretary; and Willard Gay, treasurer.

In 1867, at the Universal Exposition in Paris, Wood's machines were awarded the First Premium and The Cross of the Legion of Honor. It was the only such award given to any mowing machine shown at the Exposition.

Wood then went to Europe, where the Emperor Napoleon III conferred on the former blacksmith the title, "Sir Walter A. Wood, Chevalier of the Legion of Honor".

In 1866, the old WCP reported the W.A. Wood "mowing machine shop going full steam---turns out a new machine every 14 minutes."

The WCP of 1868 reported Wood's honor in France. Noted that Wood brought out his machine 14 yr. ago (1854). In 1868 the "great works" in Hoosick Falls was turning out 16-17,000 machines a month., and the machines were in use around the Globe.

That May the Post reported that the works created a new machine for every 10 hrs. of labor. By July it was one for every 5 1/2 hrs. of labor.

The expansion of Wood's operation created a real estate boom in Hoosick Falls. The Post reported 200 plus building lots sold that spring alone.

MORE EXPANSION

At this time the company again had to expand to meet orders. To do this Wood again bought out a neighbor business in order to use its facilities. This time it was The Caledonian Cotton Mills of C.H. Merritt and Sons, located on the south side of the Hoosick. The price of $65,000 translates to $1.5 Million in modern inflated currency.

The WCP reported on Wood's purchase in February, 1868, noting that it secured him the exclusive right to the waterpower of Hoosick falls on both sides of the river.

He was expected to convert the mills to machine shops, thereby making the Hoosick Falls works the largest mowing machine co. in the United States.

On March 26, 1870, fire again struck the north side of the river, destroying the large shop, blacksmith shop, foundry, office, store house and five dwellings that had been constructed since the 1860 blaze.

When he saw he couldn't save the north bank, and while the fires still burned, Wood set up plans for a temporary operation. Men went immediately to the woods and began felling trees. Within two weeks from the night of the fire, buildings were up and 100 machines a day were pouring from the manufactory.

After the orders were filled, a new shop was started on the north bank of the Hoosick. To make room for an even larger plant, Wood bought and had torn down two story brick buildings and three frame residences.

The new shop was 403 ft. long and 150 ft. wide. It was of single story, brick construction. It was divided into five rooms, a machine shop, a blacksmith shop, a saw shop, a setting up (or assembly) shop and a paint shop.

FIRE PROTECTION

Each room was set off by a floor to ceiling partition of brick to block the spread of fire. In addition, the rooms were united by fire-proof doors. The building was heated by steam and had gas lights. To build it, 1.6 million bricks were fired. Its self-supporting roof was said to be one of the largest of its kind in the Country. Into the roof went 350,000 board feet of lumber and 15 tons of bolts. There where three decks to the roof. For ventilation, primarily, but also to help illuminate the vast interior, there were rows of windows between the decks, 368 windows in all.

The roof was then covered with tin. Seven hundred squares were secured with two tons of solder.

John G. Peters was the designer of the roof. Darroch and Burtis, a Hoosick Falls firm, contracted to build it.

The first room on the south end of the building housed the machine shop. There were 12,000 feet of floor space, in the shape of an "L". The corner that would have made it square was partitioned off as a separate shop. It was in that first room that rough metal was processed. "The main line of shafting was connected to the wheel Dec. 6, 1870, and is one of the prettiest running lines in the state," wrote the Rensselaer County Standard. It was 300 ft. long. The belt took the hides of 50 heads of cattle to manufacture, at a cost of $2,000 ($40,000 modern).

J.A. Wilson was foreman in the Machine Shop, with Jerome Gill, asst. W.H. Slocum was timekeeper. Employed in that one room were 165 workers.

The Blacksmith Shop was 91 ft. long and 75 ft. wide. It contained fires at 32 forges. Eight were huge, circular forges in the center of the room. Machines included one large drop, one bolt making machine, three dead stroke hammers, two ponderous shears, a punch and a trip hammer.

LITTLE BY HAND

Next was the "Saw Shop". It was 91 ft. wide and 150 ft. long, and containedsaws, planers, boring machines and formers, needed to shape woodwork. Very little hand labor was required in this phase of production, when compared to "a few years ago", wrote the Standard reporter. Charles J. Tuttle was foreman, over 63 men.

Next was the "Setting up Shop", where the machines were assembled. It was 150 ft. long and 65 ft. wide. After each machine was assembled, it was tested. George A. Willis was foreman of 48 employees.

The Paint Shop was one of the largest rooms, measuring 150 by 108 ft. Here the machines were painted, touched up and packed for shipping. Foreman was Isaac A. Allen. H. Lippencott was timekeeper. Sixty were employed in the Paint Shop.

The two story structure south of the main shop was the Storehouse, "where all orders for extras are filled". The second floor was the Pattern Shop.

To the east was a three story building. It contained the grinding room and a shop where the sickles were hardened and tempered. W.P. Harwood was foreman. The shop employed 25 workmen.

On the second floor was drilling, plating, punching and stamping sections. C.C. Spencer, the foreman, used 15 men.

On the third floor was the Sickle Room. There the sickles were cut, polished and riveted to sickle bars. George T. Breese was foreman. Twelve were employed.

THREE FURNACES

The Foundry was east of the three story Sickle Shop. It was built like the main shop, except that the roof was only two decks and slated, rather than plated. The Foundry building was 396 ft. long, a third longer than a modern football field. It was 83 ft. -wide. There were 150 doors, to assure good ventilation. There were three furnaces, vented by three cupolas. The interior walls were whitewashed.

The Foundry building contained sliding cranes, erected over the floors to lift large flasks of molten metal and to remove large castings.

The Foundry could melt 50 tons of iron ore a day. When the Standard reporter visited, the plant was operating below capacity, melting 35 tons a day.

East of the Foundry was the Sand Room. It had a capacity of 900 tons. S.W. Stewart was foreman, with D. Dracy assistant. George W. Emerson was foreman of the core makers, whose job it was to create sand molds for the casting. Camp Keller was timekeeper. This critical phase of the operation employed 195 workmen.

In the east end of the Foundry, 20 ft. was partitioned off. This was the Barrel Room. It contained 18 monstrous iron cylinders or barrels. These were used in the cleaning of sand from the castings after the castings had cooled enough to be brought from the Foundry. Eight workmen were employed here. Camp Keller was also foreman.

THE LARGEST

The largest building east of the Foundry was The Scratch Shop. Here all castings were cleaned, weighed and made ready for the machine shop. Here great driving wheels powered specially designed large drills. Thirty-three men were employed. Camp Keller was also foreman of this process. F. Gale was in charge ofweighing the castings.

This Scratch Shop building, plus two engine houses (for steam had largely replaced water power by 1874, plus an office, "Comprises all of the buildings connected with this mammoth manufactory".

A switch track from the Troy and Boston Railroad connected the plant to the outside world.

Superintendent of the whole Works was J.M. Rosebrooks.

Wrote the Standard reporter, "That these (Wood mowing and reaping) machines continue to take the lead may be inferred from the fact that at the Universal Exposition at Vienna last year they were again awarded the highest prize, it being The Grand Diploma of Honor, the first and only prize on mowers and reapers in ;the gift of the Vienna Exhibition".

SIR WALTER

On December 13, 1871, the Emperor of Austria conferred upon Sir Walter A. Wood the Knights Cross of the Imperial Order of Francis Joseph.

In 1874, the Walter A. Wood company employed 700 workers, with a monthly average payroll of $40,000 ($800,000 is a very conservative estimate, in modern money).

The yearly consumption of raw material: 6,000 tons of cast iron, 1,000 tons of wrought iron, 4,000 tons of malleable iron, 100 tons of steel, 80,000 lb. brass, and 3,000,000 board ft. of lumber.

In the previous season (1873), the mowing machine works in Hoosick Falls turned out 20,715 machines. To that point, the statistical record showed 190,183 machines made and sold.

Newly elected trustees (1874): W.A. Wood, J. Russell Parsons, William B. Tibbitts, Willard Gay, T.W. Tillinghast. Officers were W. A. Wood, president; J. Russell Parsons, vice president; A.C. Green, secretary; Willard Gay, treasurer; John B. Gale, attorney. Executive Committee: Walter A. Wood, Willard Gay and C.W. Tillinghast.

In 1874, James H. Livingston published The Rensselaer County Standard. His editorial comment that January: "It is generally acknowledged by all classes of our inhabitants, from the very unthinking to the most wise, that Wood's mowing and reaping machine company are the very life and sustenance of this, our beautiful village.

"Beginning at the lowest round in the ladder of success, at a time when the great heads of the firm, Walter A. Wood and J. Russell Parsons, worked at the forge and turned out with their own hands those labor-saving harvesting machines which have gained a fame as great as any other, this company has gradually risen to a magnitude which defies the competition of the combined world!"

THE VISION

Livingston went on to speak of world fame brought to the Village, and of being situated "upon a pure, swift and valuable stream of water... one of the largest manufacturing establishments in the Country.

"...We do not deem it even a flight of the imagination to predict a great and glorious future for the Village of Hoosick Falls.

"It is a moral certainty--- a dead reckoning."

He noted that the Foundry had beenbuilt during a period of national depression. This came in the early 1870s, as the Union's huge Civil War debt greatly inflated the currency.

Walter A. Wood also supported the Band. The Hoosick Falls Cornet Band serenaded Wood on a Friday night, and "Sir Walter" came out and gave them $300 ($6,000 modern) to buy "a new outfit in the shape of uniform".

In another month the band had converted to become the "Mower and Reaping Machine Band". Wood was also mentioned as a candidate for Congress.

UNION MOVEMENT

That summer the Co. had labor problems. The Union Molders tried a strike, but "it was decided in favor of the company and business is back to normal." "Sir Walter" imported 40-50 molders from Boston and fired the union men.

"Most of the latter are now leaving the Falls area and seeking employment elsewhere."

Wood so effectively broke the Molders' Union that it disbanded, giving the office furniture to five remaining members.

The mist of time dims the brutality of the conflict, which is brought into stark focus by the fact that one of W.A. Wood's beautiful carriage horses was caught in the night and viciously mutilated.

The D and H spur at the Wood Works was so extensive it was referred to as W.A. Wood's "private railroad".

The Great
Shipment!

At the dawn of the 20th Century, on May 14, 1901 the Walter A. Wood Mowing and Reaping Machine Works sent off the greatest single shipment in its illustrious history. Onto Wood's "private railroad" were loaded 58 cars of machinery, going from Hoosick Falls to Chicago.

The train contained 3,000 harvesting machines, which, should they have been placed end to end, would have stretched five miles.

The shipping weight was 1.67 million lbs. The freight charges alone were $9,692 ($204,000 modern).

The value of the machines was $125,000 ($2.5 million modern).

2 DAYS TO CHICAGO

The train left the Falls decorated with flags and bunting. It would take 2 running days to reach Chicago, as it was allowed to run only during daylight, for the publicity value, and it paused at strategic cities for ceremonies.

In Hoosick Falls, stores and factories closed, whistles blew, bells pealed and cannon boomed.

Of the 58 cars of harvesters, 7 cars went to Illinois, 4 to Missouri, 9 to Nebraska, 7 to Iowa, 8 to Minnesota, 9 to South Dakota, one to Wisconsin, 12 to Kansas and 1 to North Dakota.

A Cambridge Connection

In 1936 George W. Peters, lived on Spring St. in Cambridge. He was most widely known as a sign painter, having long established his reputation by going through the region hand painting huge, Cambridge Fair signs on barns.

But George Peters, to quote the popular editor Charles John Stevenson, was "A sign painter in the same sensethat Henry Ford is a machinist".

Stevenson discovered Peters' cache of paintings, hidden away in his domicile. They marked him an artist of the first class, thought Stevenson.

The native of Hoosick Falls had started painting when eight years old.

When Peters was 15, he went to work for the W.A. Wood Mowing Machine Co. Wood took Peters to the state fair, as a part of the company exhibit.

At the Fair, Peters was billed as the "Lightning Artist!" He painted a landscape in 40 seconds.

The company gave away hundreds as souvenirs. It was water with sail boats and a lighthouse. A good likeness, Stevenson thought.

Seed packets from the JB Rice Seed Packet Co. Prepared exclusively for the JB Rice Co.

Aerial view, JB Rice Seed Co., Cambridge, NY

Early scenes of seed harvesting, JB Rice Seed Co. collection, OCARC

The Cambridge

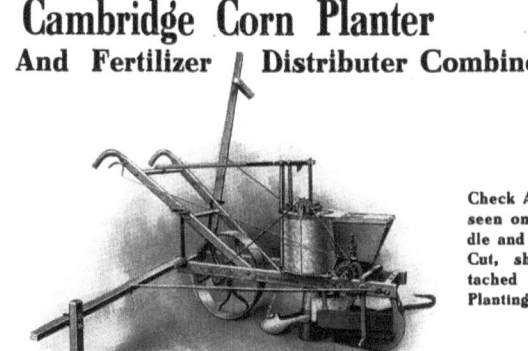

No. 29, Steel
Reversible Plow
Complete with
Automatic Jointer

Cambridge Corn Planter
And Fertilizer   Distributer Combined

Check Attachm
seen on Plante
dle and Frame
Cut, should
tached only
Planting in Che

THE LOVEJOY COMPANY

"Cambridge" Potato Digger

The "Cambridge" Potato Digger is the most successful digger on the market, constructed of first quality grey iron and malleable with soft center steel point and improved high carbon endless steel elevator chain.

This digger successfully separates the potatoes from the vines and weeds, the potatoes being delivered behind the machine in a narrow row on clean ground, while the vines are carried to the left side; the upper set of rods doing this work with the aid of

www.ingramcontent.com/pod-product-compliance
Lightning Source LLC
Chambersburg PA
CBHW040836180526
45159CB00001B/207